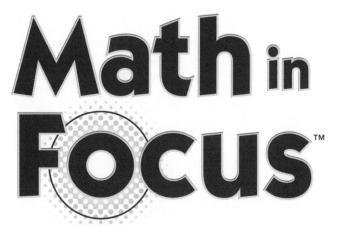

Math in Focus™

The Singapore Approach

Enrichment

3B

Consultant and Author
Dr. Fong Ho Kheong

Author
Ang Kok Cheng

Marshall Cavendish
Education

GREAT SOURCE®

HOUGHTON MIFFLIN HARCOURT
Supplemental Publishers

© 2009 Marshall Cavendish International (Singapore) Private Limited

Published by Marshall Cavendish Education
An imprint of Marshall Cavendish International (Singapore) Private Limited
A member of Times Publishing Limited

Marshall Cavendish International (Singapore) Private Limited
Times Centre, 1 New Industrial Road
Singapore 536196
Tel: +65 6411 0820
Fax: +65 6266 3677
E-mail: fps@sg.marshallcavendish.com
Website: www.marshallcavendish.com/education/sg

Distributed by
Great Source
A division of Houghton Mifflin Harcourt Publishing Company
181 Ballardvale Street
P.O. Box 7050
Wilmington, MA 01887-7050
Tel: 1-800-289-4490
Website: www.greatsource.com

First published 2009

Math in Focus ™ is a trademark of Times Publishing Limited.

Great Source ® is a registered trademark of Houghton Mifflin Harcourt Publishing Company.

Math in Focus Enrichment 3B
ISBN 978-0-669-01579-9

Printed in Singapore

1 2 3 4 5 6 7 8 MCI 16 15 14 13 12 11 10 09

Contents

Introducing

Math in Focus™

Enrichment

Written to complement *Math in Focus™: The Singapore Approach* Grade 3, exercises in *Enrichment 3A* and *3B* are designed for advanced students seeking a challenge beyond the exercises and questions in the Student Books and Workbooks.

These exercises require children to draw on their fundamental mathematical understanding as well as recently acquired concepts and skills, combining problem-solving strategies with critical thinking skills.

Critical thinking skills enhanced by working on *Enrichment* exercises include classifying, comparing, sequencing, analyzing parts and whole, identifying patterns and relationships, induction (from specific to general), deduction (from general to specific), and spatial visualization.

One set of problems is provided for each chapter, to be assigned after the chapter has been completed. *Enrichment* exercises can be assigned while other students are working on the Chapter Review/Test, or while the class is working on subsequent chapters.

BLANK

10 Money

PROBLEM SOLVING
Thinking Skills

Solve.

1. What is the difference between the greatest and the least results?

| $18.25 − $6.50 | $15.50 + $1.25 |

| $9.76 + $9.04 | $25.70 − $19.80 | $4.25 + $12.50 |

2. Fill in the boxes.

```
  $   3   4  . ☐   0
− $  ☐   9  . 0     ☐
─────────────────────
  $       5  . 3   2
```

Solve. Show your work.

3.   Sydney has 8 coins in his pocket.
The total value of the 8 coins is $1.20.
What are the coins that Sydney has?

4.   Isaac buys a block of cheese for $5.70, a bottle of olive oil for $11.25,
and a package of frozen chicken wings for $18.99.
Isaac gives the cashier three $10 bills, two $5 bills, and four $1 bills.
How much change will Isaac get in return?

PROBLEM SOLVING
Strategies

Solve. Show your work.

5. Mr. Lim buys a sweater, a handbag, and a watch.
The sweater costs $108.90.
The handbag costs $60.30 less than the sweater.
The watch costs $50.50 more than the sweater.
Mr. Lim receives $33.10 in change.
How much did Mr. Lim pay the cashier?

6. Felipe has $84.70.
Carter has $12.75 less than Felipe.
Diana has $16.40 more than Carter.
How much do the three of them have altogether?

7.   Ava buys a chair and two identical stools at a sale for $70.
The price difference between the chair and the two stools is $30.
What is the total cost of the chair and one stool?

PROBLEM SOLVING
Exploration

Solve using two methods.

8. $8.70 + $5.85

9. $26.50 − $7.85

Journal Writing

**Add mentally. First add the dollars and then add the cents.
List the steps you use.**

10. $5.25 + $4.00 = _____

   | Step 1 | _____ |

   | Step 2 | _____ |

   | Step 3 | _____ |

11. $7.40 + $0.35 = _____

   | Step 1 | _____ |

   | Step 2 | _____ |

   | Step 3 | _____ |

12. $4.85 + $11.50 = _____

   | Step 1 | _____ |

   | Step 2 | _____ |

   | Step 3 | _____ |

**Add mentally. Use the 'add and then subtract' strategy.
List the steps you use.**

13. $8.40 + $0.85 = _____

> Step 1   _____

> Step 2   _____

14. $9.65 + $7.75 = _____

> Step 1   _____

> Step 2   _____

**Subtract mentally. First subtract the dollars and then subtract the cents.
List the steps you use.**

15. $12.75 − $0.30 = _____

> Step 1   _____

> Step 2   _____

> Step 3   _____

16. $76.60 − $32.25 = _____

> Step 1   _____

> Step 2   _____

> Step 3   _____

Subtract mentally. First subtract whole dollars and then add the extra cents. List the steps you use.

17. $15.40 − $0.75 = _____

     Step 1   _____

     Step 2   _____

18. $78.30 − $5.65 = _____

     Step 1   _____

     Step 2   _____

CHAPTER 11 Metric Length, Mass, and Volume

PROBLEM SOLVING
Thinking Skills

Solve.

1. Victoria jogged 1 kilometer 600 meters on Monday.
Find the distance she jogged in centimeters.

Read the scale.

2. What is the mass of the sugar in grams?

3.   Express the volume of water in the jug in milliliters.

Follow the directions.

4.   Estimate the length of the stick in centimeters.

200 cm

stick

5.   Find the height of the fish tank in centimeters.

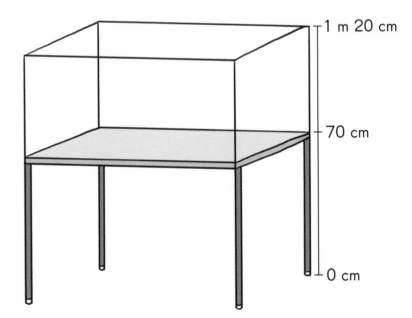

The height of the fish tank is _____ centimeters.

6. Emma finds the mass of a bag and a chair.
She finds that the bag has a mass of 6 kilograms 9 grams.
Both the chair and the bag have the same mass.
Color the boxes that show the mass of the chair.

6,090 g	6,900 g	6,009 g
6 kg 9 g	6 kg 900 g	6 kg 90 g

7. A jug contains 3 liters 500 milliliters of water.
Water from the jug is used to fill seven 250-milliliter mugs.
Find the amount of water left in the jug.

8. Convert each measurement to liters and milliliters.
Then shade the boxes with the two largest and the two smallest measurements.

Y	S	O	E
1,903 mL	6,012 mL	3,250 mL	7,009 mL
____ L ____ mL	____ L ____ mL	____ L ____ mL	____ L ____ mL

J	T	D	R
300 mL	1 mL	4,020 mL	1,025 mL
____ L ____ mL	____ L ____ mL	____ L ____ mL	____ L ____ mL

A	I	U	M
5,001 mL	8,150 mL	6,905 mL	250 mL
____ L ____ mL	____ L ____ mL	____ L ____ mL	____ L ____ mL

Arrange the letters in the shaded boxes to spell out the answer to the following riddle.

What can fly without wings?

_____ _____ _____ _____

Strategies

9.   Look for the pattern.
Then fill in the missing masses.

50 g   100 g   200 g   _____   550 g   800 g   _____

PROBLEM SOLVING
Exploration

**Study the diagram showing the distances between cities.
Then follow the directions.**

10.   Rita wants to fly from City A to City P.
There is no direct flight from City A to City P.

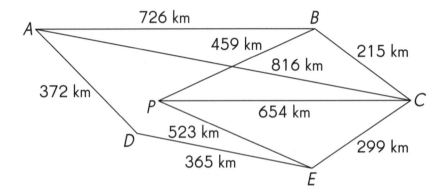

AB = 726 km	BC = 215 km	AC = 816 km
BP = 459 km	PC = 654 km	PE = 523 km
CE = 299 km	AD = 372 km	DE = 365 km

Find five ways to travel from City A to City P indirectly.
Choose the best route.
Explain why you chose that route.

11.   The total mass of two goats is 48 kilograms.
The mass of one of the goats is at least 10 kilograms more
than the other.
The mass of the lighter goat is more than 16 kilograms.
Find three possible masses of the heavier goat.

 Journal Writing

Correct the mistakes.

12. 2 km 5 cm = 2 × 100 cm + 5 cm = 205 cm

_____

_____

13. 4,050 g = 40 kg 50 g

_____

_____

14. 750 mL = 7 L 50 mL

_____

_____

15. You are given 4 coins.
One of the coins is fake and is lighter than the other 3 coins.
List the steps that you could use to find out which coin is fake.

Step 1 _____

_____

Step 2 _____

_____

12 Real-World Problems: Measurement

Thinking Skills

Solve.

1. Lucas is 136 centimeters tall.
    Aiden is 25 centimeters shorter than Lucas.
    Eric is 14 centimeters taller than Aiden.
    How tall is Eric?
    Give your answer in meters and centimeters.

2. A car is crossing a bridge.
    The bridge is 62 meters 36 centimeters long.
    The car has traveled 34 meters 54 centimeters from one
    end of the bridge.
    Find the distance the car must travel to reach the other
    end of the bridge.

3.   The mass of a can full of paint is 7 kilograms 400 grams.
           When half of the paint is poured out, the total mass of the can
           is 4 kilograms.
           What is the mass of the empty can?

4.   A jug can hold 550 milliliters of water.
           A pail can hold 5 times as much water as the jug.
           What is the capacity of the jug and the pail altogether?
           Give your answer in liters and milliliters.

5.   A suitcase has a mass of ☐ .

What is the mass of the suitcase?

◎ + ☐ + ☐ = 62 kg

◎ − ☐ − ☐ = 30 kg

6.   Xavier jogs from Point A to Point C.
After resting for half an hour, he decides to walk back from
Point C to Point B.
Then he continues jogging from Point B to Point A.
How far does Xavier jog in all?
Give your answer in meters.

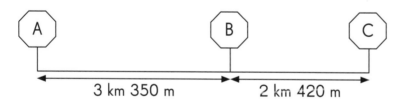

A   B   C

3 km 350 m   2 km 420 m

7.   John sells 3 liters 596 milliliters of lemonade on Monday.
He sells 679 milliliters less on Tuesday than on Monday and
some more on Wednesday.
John sells a total of 8 liters of lemonade during the three days.
How much lemonade does he sell on Wednesday?

PROBLEM SOLVING
Strategies

Solve.

8.   The length of a road is 80 meters.
Streetlamps are placed on both sides of the road.
The streetlamps are equally spaced along the road a distance of
8 meters apart.
How many streetlamps are placed along the road if both ends of the
road have streetlamps?

9.   There was some water in a tank.
Matilda uses some of the water from the tank to completely fill
4 empty bottles. Each bottle has a capacity of 500 milliliters.
She then uses 16 liters to water her garden.
Matilda is left with a quarter of the original amount of water in the tank.
How much water was there in the tank at first?

10. There are 3 iron bars and 4 metal pipes in a container.
The mass of each iron bar is 2 kilograms more than the mass of each metal pipe.
The total mass of the container and the items is 66 kilograms.
The container weighs 4 kilograms. Find the mass of one iron bar and the mass of one metal pipe.

11. Owen and Hunter have a mass of 135 kilograms altogether.
Hunter and Devin have a mass of 68 kilograms altogether.
Owen's mass is twice as much as Hunter's mass.
What is Devin's mass?

12. At a charity walk, Bryan walks 3 kilometers 320 meters more than Luis. Kerry walks 850 meters less than Bryan.
Luis walks 6 kilometers. Find the total distance walked by Kerry and Bryan.

PROBLEM SOLVING
Exploration

Write word problems using the bar models given.

13.   Write a one-step word problem and a two-step word problem.
Then solve the problems.

2 cm

24 cm

14.   Write a two-step word problem.
Then solve the problem.

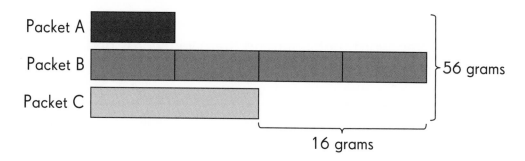

Journal Writing

15. Write a one-step word problem using the given words and numbers. Then solve the problem.

Augusta	bottle	jug	milk	725 mL
248 mL	pours	left	at first	

16. Write a two-step word problem using the given words and numbers. Then solve the problem.

Bradley	Casper	meat	sell	left	4 times
altogether	25 kg	7 kg	at first		

13 Bar Graphs and Line Plots

PROBLEM SOLVING
Thinking Skills

The bar graph shows the number of pies Mrs. Davis baked during four days.
Use the data in the bar graph to complete Exercises 1 to 3.

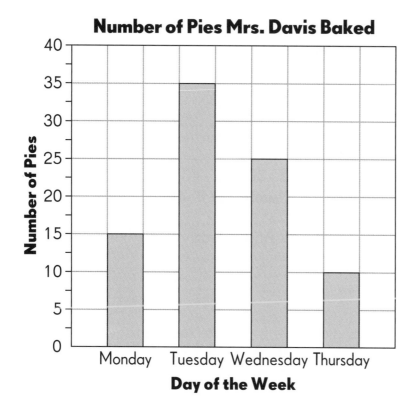

1. Mrs. Davis baked _____ more pies on Wednesday than on Thursday.

2.   She baked _____ fewer pies on Monday than on Tuesday.

3.   She baked a total of _____ pies from Monday through Wednesday.

The bar graph shows the number of books read by four students in a month. Use the data in the bar graph to answer Exercises 4 to 6.

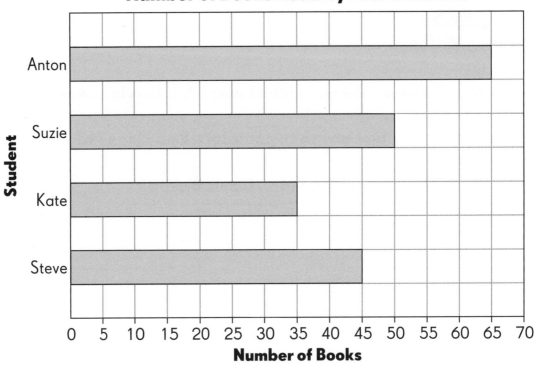

Number of Books Read by Four Students

4.   How many books did Steve and Anton read altogether?

_____ books

5.   How many more books did Suzie and Kate read altogether than Steve?

_____ books

6.   If Steve stacks all the books he read into 5 equal groups, how many books will there be in each stack?

_____ books

The table shows the number of students in each class.

Class	Number of Students
3A	14
3B	26
3C	12
3D	18
3E	20

7. Complete the bar graph.
Use the data in the table.

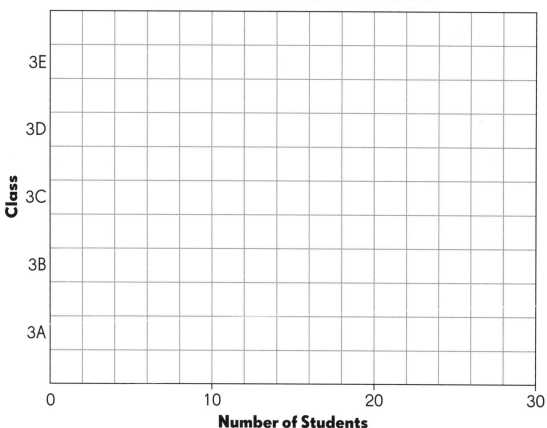

Number of Students in Each Class

Answer Exercises 8 to 10.
Use the data in the bar graph.

8. If all the students are asked to stand in rows of 10 people, how many rows will there be?

_____ rows

9. Each student in class 3A and class 3C drinks one carton of milk at lunch. How many cartons of milk will the school need to order for class 3A and class 3C altogether?

_____ cartons

10. All the students in class 3C and class 3E, and 5 students from class 3D are asked to clean the school hall and the cafeteria after school. How many students will be staying after school to clean?

_____ students

The picture graph shows the number of pancakes Sofia sold during the first two days of a fair.

Pancakes Sofia Sold

Strawberry	◯ ◯ ◯ ◯ ◯
Chocolate	◯ ◯ ◯ ◯ ◯ ◯ ◯ ◯
Buttermilk	◯ ◯ ◯
Banana	◯ ◯

Key: Each ◯ stands for 5 pancakes.

11. Complete the bar graph.
Use the data in the picture graph.

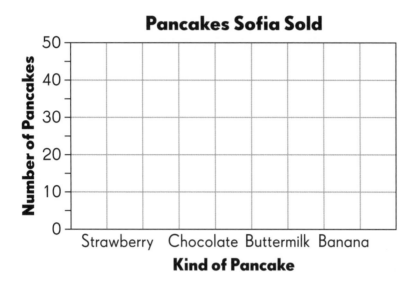

Pancakes Sofia Sold

Answer Exercises 12 to 14.
Use the data in the bar graph.

12. How many more buttermilk pancakes must Sofia sell to reach her goal of selling 48 buttermilk pancakes?

_____ buttermilk pancakes

13. Sofia sells each strawberry pancake for $3 and each chocolate pancake for $2.
Does she earn more from the sale of strawberry pancakes or chocolate pancakes?

14. Sofia needs to sell 155 pancakes altogether in order to reach her goal. How many more pancakes does she need to sell?

The tally chart shows the number of pencils Rebecca's friends have.

15. Complete the tally chart.

Number of Pencils	Tally	Number of Friends
1	~~||||~~ |||	
2	~~||||~~	
3	~~||||~~ ~~||||~~ ~~||||~~		
4	~~||||~~ ||	
5	~~||||~~ ~~||||~~ ||	

16. Complete the line plot that Rebecca started.

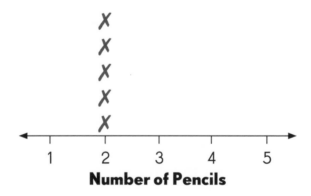

Number of Pencils

Key: Each ✗ stands for 1 friend.

Complete Exercises 17 to 19.
Use the data in the line plot.

17. How many of Rebecca's friends have more than 3 pencils?

_____ friends

18. There are _____ more friends who have 5 pencils than 2 pencils.

19. How many of her friends have 1, 2, or 3 pencils?

_____ friends

PROBLEM SOLVING
Strategies

Solve.

20. The line plot follows a pattern.
How many **X**s will there be for 6 marbles?

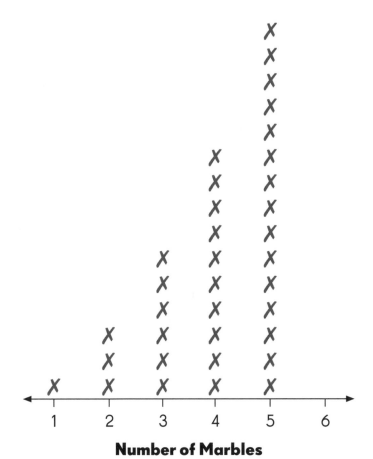

Number of Marbles

Gillian goes to the market and buys some eggs.
After saving some eggs for the week, she has 12 eggs left.

21. Read the information given and complete the bar graph.
Then find out how many eggs Gillian buys from the market.

Number of eggs Gillian saved for the week:
- 3 eggs for Wednesday.
- For Monday, 2 more eggs than she saved for Wednesday.
- For Thursday, 4 fewer eggs than she saved for Monday.
- Twice as many eggs for Tuesday than for Thursday.
- The same number of eggs for Tuesday and Friday.

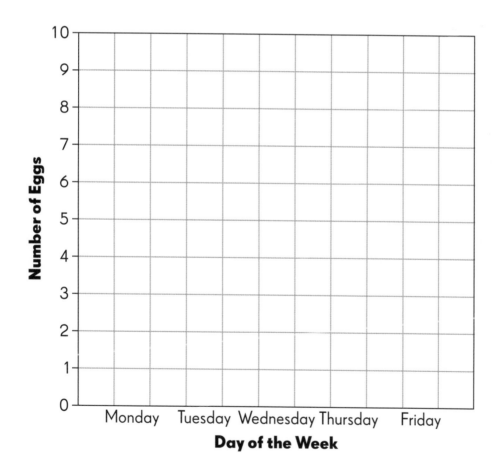

Gillian buys _____ eggs from the market.

PROBLEM SOLVING
Exploration

The table shows the different kinds of transportation that students take to school.

Kind of Transportation	Number of Students
Bicycle	12
Car	26
School bus	38
Walk	18

Use the data in the table to draw two different bar graphs.

22.

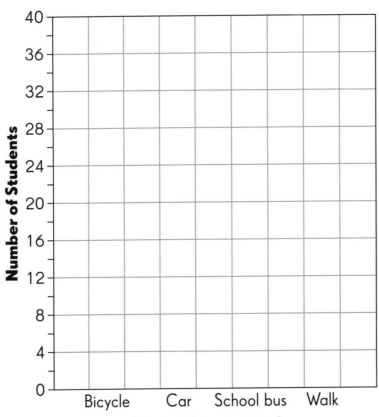

23.

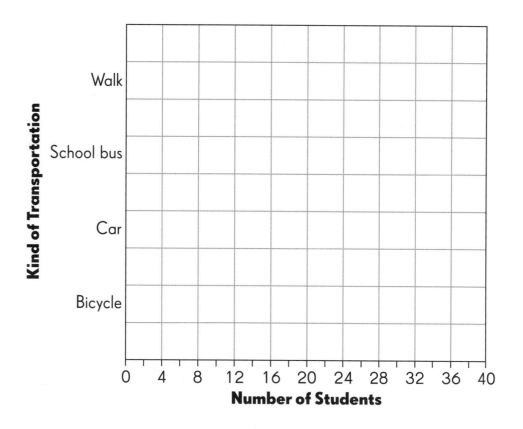

The bar graph shows the amount of money spent by four friends.
Use the bar graph to complete Exercises 24 to 26.

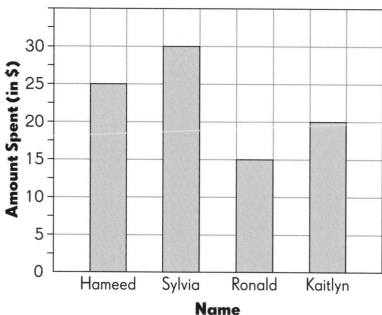

24. How many of the friends spent more than $24?

_____ friends

25. Who spent the most amount of money?

_____

26. How much more money must Hameed spend so that he spends twice as much as Ronald?

$_____

Journal Writing

The bar graph shows the number of muffins Bruce baked from Monday through Thursday.

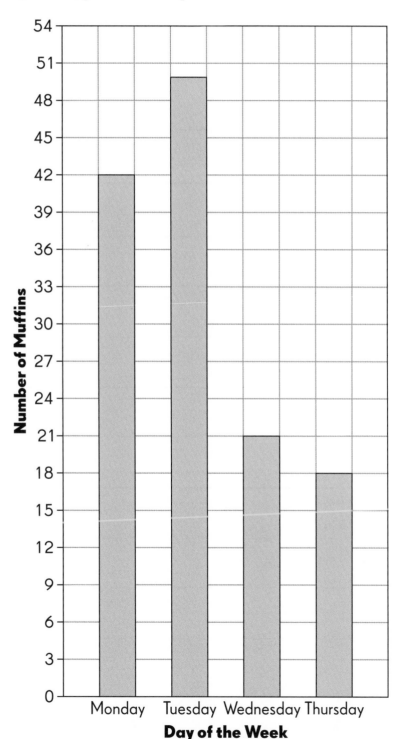

27. Write four questions that can be answered by the bar graph.
Use the words in the box.
Then answer the questions.

> more than   less than   altogether   as many as
>
> twice   most   least

Question 1: _____

_____

Answer : _____

Question 2: _____

_____

Answer: _____

Question 3: _____

_____

Answer: _____

Question 4: _____

_____

Answer: _____

Fractions

PROBLEM SOLVING

Thinking Skills

Solve.

1. Circle the fractions that are not equivalent to $\frac{1}{4}$.

> $\frac{6}{12}$ $\frac{3}{12}$ $\frac{2}{6}$ $\frac{4}{12}$ $\frac{2}{8}$

2. Compare the fractions in the squares.
Shade the squares that have a fraction greater than $\frac{1}{2}$.

$\frac{6}{9}$	$\frac{2}{10}$	$\frac{1}{4}$
$\frac{4}{12}$	$\frac{2}{8}$	$\frac{3}{10}$
$\frac{6}{10}$	$\frac{4}{4}$	$\frac{11}{12}$
$\frac{1}{8}$	$\frac{5}{7}$	$\frac{4}{5}$

3.   What is the difference between the fraction of unshaded parts and the fraction of shaded parts?

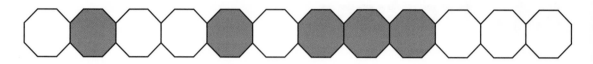

4.   Put the numbers 12, 1, 4, 6, 2 and 8 in the boxes to make three equivalent fractions.

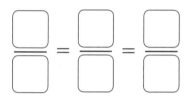

5.   The figure is divided into equal parts.

How many more parts need to be shaded to have $\frac{3}{4}$ of the figure shaded?

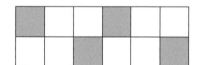

6.   Jennifer paints $\frac{1}{2}$ of a pole red and $\frac{5}{12}$ of it yellow. What fraction of the pole is not painted?

PROBLEM SOLVING
Strategies

Solve.

7. Write the missing fraction in the pattern.

$$\frac{1}{12}, \quad \frac{1}{9}, \quad \frac{1}{8}, \quad \frac{1}{6}, \quad \boxed{}, \quad \frac{1}{3}$$

8. Brenda cuts a pie into several equal slices.
She gives Sally 2 slices of the pie. Peter takes a quarter of the pie.
Henry takes 5 slices, and Brenda is left with 2 slices.

    a. How many slices did Brenda cut the pie into?

    b. What fraction of the pie does Brenda have left?

PROBLEM SOLVING
Exploration

Follow the directions.

9. Use two methods to find the greater fraction.

$$\frac{7}{8} \qquad \frac{5}{6}$$

Method 1:

Method 2:

10. Hector picked at least $\frac{5}{9}$ of the total number of fruits picked from the trees. Sam picked 24 fruits, which is $\frac{1}{4}$ of the total number of fruits picked. What is the possible number of fruits Hector picked?

Journal Writing

Order the fractions from greatest to least.
Then list the steps you used.

11. $\dfrac{5}{8}$ $\dfrac{1}{2}$ $\dfrac{7}{12}$

Step 1 _____

Step 2 _____

Step 3 _____

Shade parts of the model to show each fraction.
Then list the steps you used.

12. $\dfrac{3}{4}$

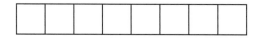

Step 1 _____

Step 2 _____

Step 3 _____

13. $\frac{6}{14}$

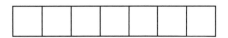

Step 1 _____

Step 2 _____

Step 3 _____

14. Jason wrote $\frac{1}{2} + \frac{1}{3} = \frac{2}{5}$.

Use estimation to show that Jason's solution cannot be correct.
Explain your reasoning.

CHAPTER 15 Customary Length, Weight, and Capacity

Thinking Skills

1. Andy is 2 inches shorter than Boyle.
   Boyle is 6 inches taller than Carla.
   Carla is 3 inches taller than Dan.
   Dan is 51 inches tall.

   Order the children from the shortest to the tallest.

_____, _____, _____, _____

shortest   tallest

2. A container can hold 3 gallons 2 quarts 4 pints of water.
A bottle can hold 4 cups of water.
How many bottles are needed to fill the container completely?

3. Each ▢ has a weight of 3 ounces and each ⬡ has a weight of 1 pound.

What is the weight of ◯?

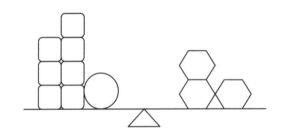

PROBLEM SOLVING
Strategies

4. A metal cupboard has a weight of 2 ◯.
What is its weight?

$$\boxed{+} + \bigcirc = 53 \text{ lb}$$

$$\boxed{-} - \bigcirc = 25 \text{ lb}$$

5. Mark mixes 1 cup of syrup with 4 cups of water to make a drink for 2 people. He has 2 quarts of syrup and 2 gallons of water. How many people will Mark be able to serve altogether?

6. Nine street lamps are placed at equal intervals along a 64-yard long footpath. How far is the 4th street lamp from the 7th?

1st

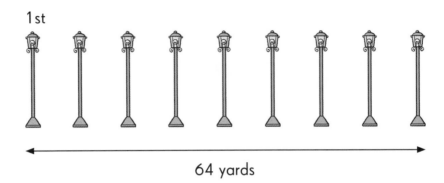

64 yards

7. Three boys take part in the school's long jump trial. Roy jumps 5 inches farther than Daniel. Daniel jumps 23 inches farther than Stuart. They jump a total distance of 177 inches. How far does Stuart jump?

8. A truck delivers sacks of flour to various destinations. Each sack weighs 3 pounds. The truck drops off 4 sacks at Point A, 6 sacks at Point B, and 2 sacks at Point C. The truck has 12 pounds of flour left for Point D. How much flour was loaded on to the truck to start with?

PROBLEM SOLVING
Exploration

9. The diagram shows how four cities are linked by different flying routes.
Find all the routes you can take to fly from City A to City C.
Find the total distance of each route.
Which route covers the longest distance?

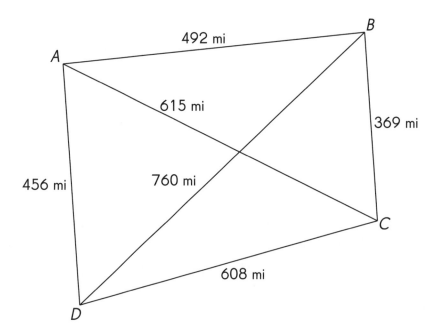

10.   A barrel contains 2 gallons of milk. Gary pours all the milk into
some containers that have capacities that are labeled in either
quarts or pints.
What are the possible combinations of containers he uses?
Show 6 possible combinations.

 Journal Writing

Find the error. Then correct the mistake.

11.   1 mile 70 yards = 1,070 yards

12.   4 gallons = 2 × 4 pints
                      = 8 pints

13.   3 pounds of meat has the same weight as 36 ounces of meat.

14. You are given three coins. One of the coins weighs 2 ounces and the other two coins weigh 3 ounces each. Explain in steps to tell which one of the three coins weighs 2 ounces.

Step 1 _____

Step 2 _____

Step 3 _____

15. Order the capacities from smallest to largest.
Then list the steps you used to order the measures.

> 1 gallon   5 pints   16 pints
>
> 7 quarts   7 pints

_____, _____, _____, _____, _____
  smallest   largest

Step 1 _____

Step 2 _____

Step 3 _____

16 Time and Temperature

PROBLEM SOLVING
Thinking Skills

1. Vanessa studies from 11:00 A.M. to 2:10 P.M.
   She rests for 45 minutes during that time.
   How long does Vanessa spend studying?

2. Jill leaves home at 1:15 P.M. She reaches the mall
   30 minutes later. After shopping for 2 hours 20 minutes,
   she takes a cab home. Jill reaches home at 5:10 P.M.
   How long is the cab ride?

3.   School starts at 8:00 A.M. Lenny spends 6 hours in school.
He swims at the pool for 1 hour 15 minutes after school. He goes home
after he is done swimming. What time does Lenny leave the pool?

4.   Ryan takes 45 minutes to run around the field.
Ryan is 20 minutes faster than Dylan. What time does
Dylan finish running if they both start at 7:30 A.M.?

The thermometers show the temperatures at different times of day. Study the thermometers and answer Exercises 5 to 8.

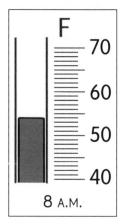
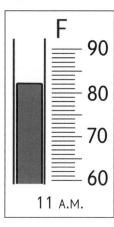
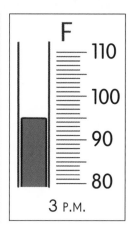
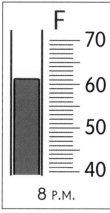
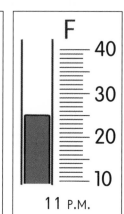

5.   What time of the day is the temperature highest?

_____

6.   What time of the day is the temperature lowest?

_____

7.   What is the greatest temperature difference?

_____

8.   How much higher is the temperature at 3 P.M. than at 11 A.M.?

_____

PROBLEM SOLVING
Strategies

9. These temperature readings were taken during the afternoon.
    If the temperature continued to follow this pattern, what would the
    temperature be at 6 P.M.?

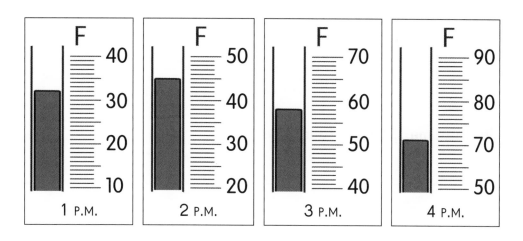

10. Suzi goes to the market with her mother. It takes them
    15 minutes to reach the market. They spend 1 hour 10 minutes there
    before heading to the food mall for an hour for lunch. They leave the
    food mall at 1:15 P.M. What time do they leave for the market?

PROBLEM SOLVING
Exploration

Look at the clock.

11.   Write the time shown in four ways.

_____

_____

Solve.

12.   The clock shows 1:20 P.M.
Write four possible activities you can do at this time.

_____

_____

_____

_____

13.   Jay and Jessie go to a movie.
The movie starts at 7:55 P.M. and ends at 10:15 P.M.
How long was the movie?
Give two methods to find the answer.

Method 1:

Method 2:

Journal Writing

Find the mistakes. Then write the correct statements.

14. The time shown on the clock is half past 12.

Mistake:

_____

Correct answer:

_____

15. The time shown on the clock is 7:20.

Mistake:

_____

Correct answer:

_____

Fill in the blanks.
Then list the steps used to make the conversion.

16.   3 h 45 min = _____ min

     | Step 1 | _____

     | Step 2 | _____

17.   100 min = _____ h _____ min

     | Step 1 | _____

     | Step 2 | _____

18.   255 min = _____ h _____ min

     | Step 1 | _____

     | Step 2 | _____

Angles and Lines

PROBLEM SOLVING
Thinking Skills

1.   Circle the letters that do not have angles in them.

U A E H O

Q Z T S

2.   Circle the letters that have at least four angles in them.

W A T X

F D H C

3.   How many more angles, that are greater than a right angle, can you find in Figure A than in Figure B?

Figure A   Figure B

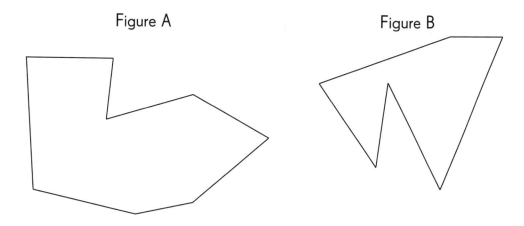

4.   Match and color the shapes that have the same number of angles in them. Use different colors for each set of shapes.

5.   How many right angles in all does the cube have?

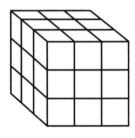

6.   The figure is made up of a square and a triangle placed side by side. Draw the figure to scale in the space provided.

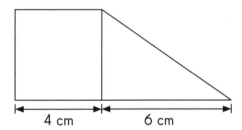

PROBLEM SOLVING
Strategies

7.   How many right angles will there be when the pattern reaches
the 10th line?

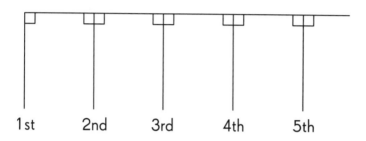

1st   2nd   3rd   4th   5th

8.   The figures are arranged in a pattern.
How many right angles will there be in Pattern 5?

Pattern 1   Pattern 2   Pattern 3

PROBLEM SOLVING
Exploration

9. Draw two 4-sided figures on the dot paper.
    Each figure must have at least one right angle.

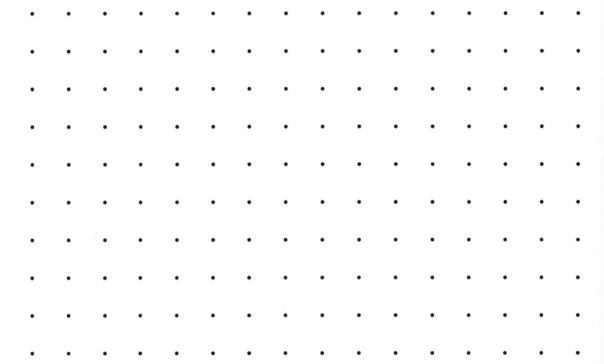

10. Draw two 4-sided figures on the dot paper.
Each figure must have an angle greater than a right angle.

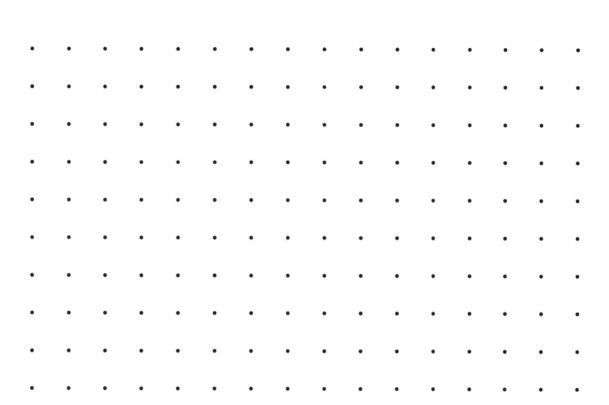

Journal Writing

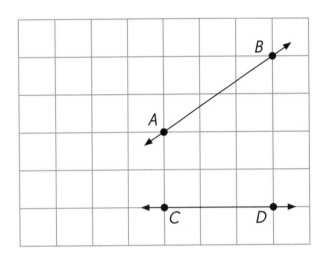

11.   Is line *AB* parallel to line *CD*? _____

12.   Give a reason for your answer. You may draw on the grid to help explain your reason.

_____

_____

_____

_____

_____

CHAPTER 18

Two-Dimensional Shapes

Thinking Skills

1. Cut out the shapes and use them to form a figure that has 6 sides.

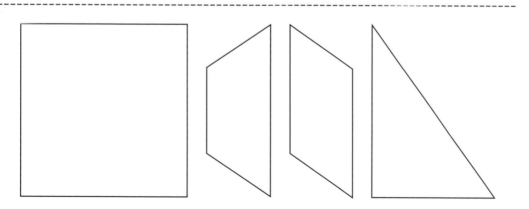

2.   Draw line segments on the polygon to show how it is formed from
1 hexagon, 2 rectangles, and 2 triangles.

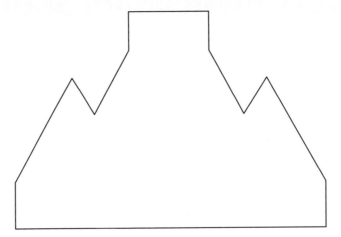

✂ -

3.   Cut out and arrange the tangram pieces to form this shape.

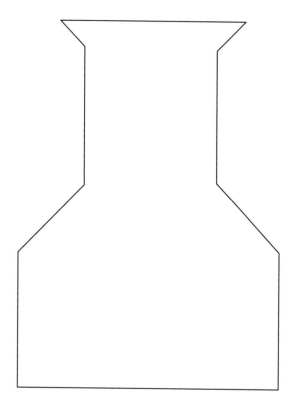

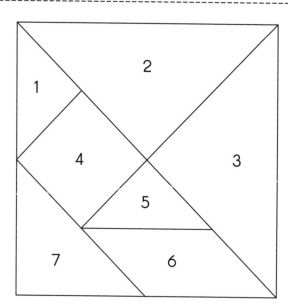

BLANK

PROBLEM SOLVING
Strategies

4.   The shape on the grid has gone through these three steps.

   Step 1   Flip the shape.

   Step 2   Rotate the shape through a half-turn to the right.

   Step 3   Slide across six squares.

   Draw the shape's original position.

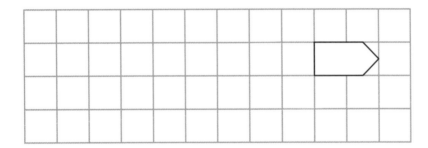

5.   The picture below is made up of hexagons laid in a pattern. How many more hexagons are required to fill in the center of the pattern?

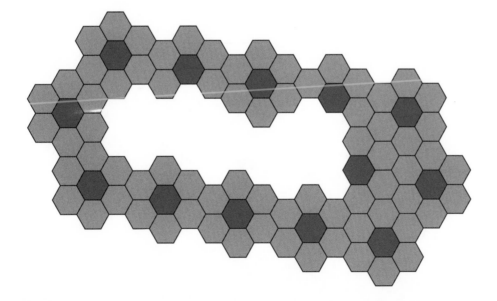

PROBLEM SOLVING
Exploration

6. Describe what each pair of quadrilaterals has in common.

   a. A rectangle and a parallelogram

   b. A trapezoid and a square

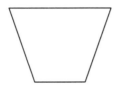   

7.   **a.**   Draw 2 figures that are congruent to the shape.

       b.   Draw 2 figures that are not congruent to the shape.

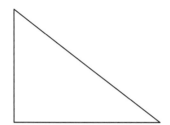

8.   Shade squares so that the dotted line becomes a line of symmetry.

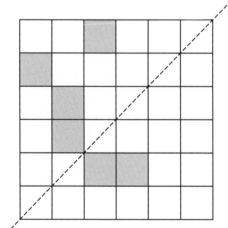

 Journal Writing

9. Explain why the statements are wrong.

   a. The figure shows a flip.

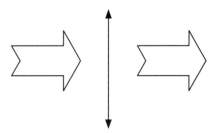

   b. The figure shows a rotation.

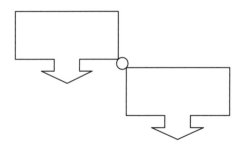

   c. The figure shows a slide.

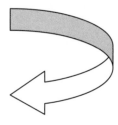 

10.   Explain why the pair of figures are not congruent.

a.

b.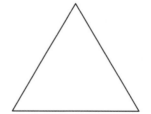

19 Area and Perimeter

PROBLEM SOLVING
Thinking Skills

1. Stuart wants to form a 10-centimeter by 4-centimeter rectangle by combining the two shapes shown below. How many more 1-centimeter squares does Stuart need to add to these shapes to form his rectangle?

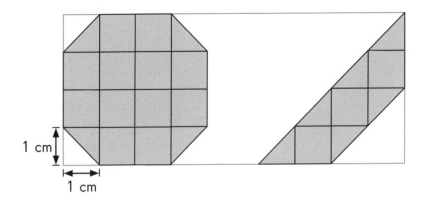

1 cm

1 cm

2. A picture is mounted onto a piece of cardboard such that it has a 5-centimeter border around it. The picture measures 10 centimeters by 8 centimeters. What will the perimeter of the cardboard be if the border is reduced by 3 centimeters on all sides?

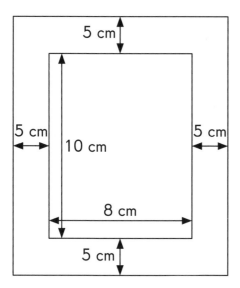

3. Amy wants to cut 2-centimeter squares from a piece of paper that measures 8 centimeters by 6 centimeters. How many squares can she cut from the paper?

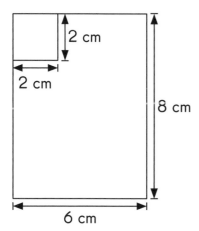

4. A square is made up of 36 1-foot squares put together as shown.
The rectangle has the same perimeter as the square.
What is the length of the rectangle?

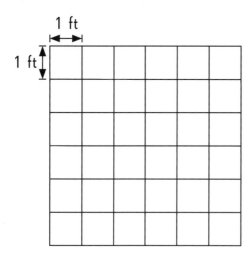

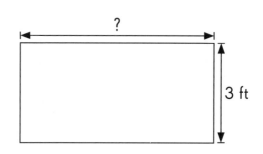

PROBLEM SOLVING
Strategies

5. A rectangle is divided into several parts. A is twice as large as B. B is twice as large as C. C is twice as large as D and D has the same area as E. The area of E is 6 square centimeters. What is the area of the whole rectangle?

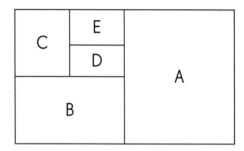

6. Tyrell makes a pattern using 1-inch squares as shown. What is the area of the 5th pattern?

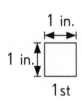

1 in.

1 in.

1st

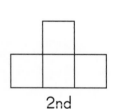

2nd

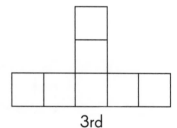

3rd

PROBLEM SOLVING
Exploration

7.   Use these squares and half-squares to make three figures.
Each figure should use all of the squares and half-squares.
Then fill in the table.

☐ ☐ ☐ ☐ ☐ ◺ ◺ ◺ ◺

Figure A   Figure B   Figure C

Figure	Number of Squares	Number of Half-Squares	Area	Perimeter
A				
B				
C				

What can you say about the areas and perimeters?

8.

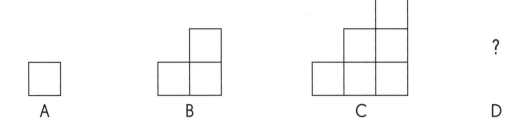

A   B   C   D

a. How many 1-centimeter squares are in each figure?

b. How many squares will be in D?

c. Do you see a pattern?

d. Using this pattern, find the number of squares in the 10th figure.

 Journal Writing

9. The length of a rectangle is 15 centimeters and the perimeter is 54 centimeters.

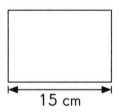

15 cm

Explain how to find the width of the rectangle.

Step 1 _____

Step 2 _____

Step 3 _____

10. The figure is made up of a square and a rectangle.

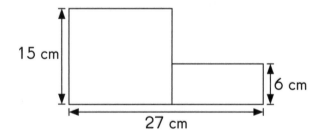

15 cm

6 cm

27 cm

Explain how to find the perimeter of the figure.

Step 1 _____

Step 2 _____

Step 3 _____

Answers

Chapter 10

1. Thinking skills: Comparing, Sequencing

   Solution:

   $18.25 − $6.50 = $11.75

   $15.50 + $1.25 = $16.75

   $9.76 + $9.04 = $18.80 ← greatest

   $25.70 − $19.80 = $5.90 ← least

   $4.25 + $12.50 = $16.75

   $18.80 − $5.90 = $12.90

2. Thinking skills: Analyzing parts and whole, Deduction

   Solution:

   ```
     $3 4. 4 0
   − $2 9. 0 8
   ─────────────
     $  5. 3 2
   ```

3. Thinking skills: Analyzing parts and whole, Deduction

   Solution:

   $0.25 + $0.25 + $0.25 + $0.25 = $1.00

   (since 5 quarters will exceed $1.20)

   The other 4 coins could be a mix of dimes and nickels. Pennies are not possible because the value of 4 pennies is only 4¢.

   We would need another 20 cents to make the total amount of $1.20.

   Therefore, it is either 2 dimes or 4 nickels. Since he has 8 coins in total, it must be 4 nickels.

   He has 4 quarters and 4 nickels.

4. Thinking skills: Analyzing parts and whole, Comparing

   Solution:

   Amount given: $10 + $10 + $10 + $5 + $5
   + $1 + $1 + $1 + $1
   = $44

   Total cost: $5.70 + $11.25 + $18.99
   = $35.94

   $44 − $35.94 = $8.06

5. Strategy: Work backward

   Solution:

   Cost of handbag: $108.90 − $60.30
   = $48.60

   Cost of watch: $108.90 + $50.50
   = $159.40

   Amount paid by Mr. Lim:

   $33.10 + $108.90 + $48.60 + $159.40
   = $350

6. Strategy: Use a model

   Solution:

   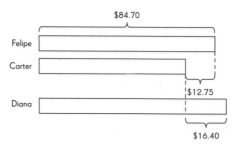

   Carter has $84.70 − $12.75 = $71.95

   Diana has $71.95 + $16.40 = $ 88.35

   Total amount = $71.95 + $88.35 + $84.70
   = $245.00

7. Strategy: Use a model

   Solution:

   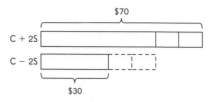

   4 units → 40

   1 unit → 40 ÷ 4 = 10

   The cost of a stool is $10.

   $70 − $10 − $10 = $50

   The cost of a chair is $50.

   $50 + $10 = $60

   The total cost of the chair and one stool is $60.

8. Answers vary.

   Sample answer:

   Method 1

   $8.70 + $6 = $14.70

   $14.70 − 15¢ = $14.55

   Method 2

   $9 + $5.85 = $14.85

   $14.85 − 30¢ = $14.55

9. Answers vary.

   Sample answer:

   Method 1

   $26.50 − $8 = $18.50

   $18.50 + 15¢ = $18.65

   Method 2

   $27 − $7.85 = $19.15

   $19.15 − 50¢ = $18.65

10. $9.25

   Step 1 $5 + $4 = $9

   Step 2 25¢ + 0¢ = 25¢

   Step 3 $9 + 25¢ = $9.25

11. $7.75

   Step 1 $7 + $0 = $7

   Step 2 40¢ + 35¢ = 75¢

   Step 3 $7 + 75¢ = $7.75

12. $16.35

   Step 1 $4 + $11 = $15

   Step 2 85¢ + 50¢ = $1.35

   Step 3 $15 + $1.35 = $16.35

13. $9.25

   Step 1 $8.40 + $1 = $9.40

   Step 2 $9.40 − 15¢ = $9.25

14. $17.40

   Step 1 $9.65 + $8 = $17.65

   Step 2 $17.65 − 25¢ = $17.40

15. $12.45

   Step 1 $12 − $0 = $12

   Step 2 75¢ − 30¢ = $0.45

   Step 3 $12 + 45¢ = $12.45

16. $44.35

   Step 1 $76 − $32 = $44

   Step 2 60¢ − 25¢ = 35¢

   Step 3 $44 + 35¢ = $44.35

17. $14.65

   Step 1 $15.40 − $1 = $14.40

   Step 2 $14.40 + 25¢ = $14.65

18. $72.65

   Step 1 $78.30 − $6 = $72.30

   Step 2 $72.30 + 35¢ = $72.65

Chapter 11

1. Thinking skill: Comparing

    Solution:

    1 m = 100 cm

    1 km = 1,000 m = 100,000 cm

    600 m = 60,000 cm

    1 km 600 m = 100,000 cm + 60,000 cm

    = 160,000 cm

2. Thinking skill: Comparing

    Solution:

    2 kg 400 g = 2,400 g

3. Thinking skill: Comparing

    Solution:

    1,700 mL

4. Thinking skill: Comparing

    Solution:

    The stick is about 50 centimeters long.

5. Thinking skill: Analyzing parts and whole

    Solution:

    120 cm − 70 cm = 50 cm

    The height of the fish tank is 50 centimeters.

6. Thinking skill: Comparing

    Solution:

    6,009 g; 6 kg 9 g

7. Thinking skill: Analyzing parts and whole

    Solution:

    Amount of water poured into the mugs:

    250 mL × 7 = 1,750 mL

    3,500 mL − 1,750 mL = 1,750 mL

    = 1 L 750 mL

    Amount of water left in the jug is 1 liter 750 milliliters.

8. Thinking skills: Comparing, Sequencing

    Solution:

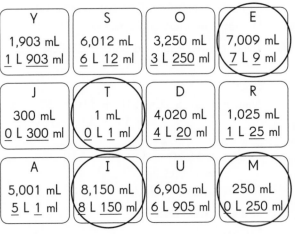

    TIME

9. Strategy: Look for patterns

    350 g; 1,100 g

10. Strategy: Make a list

Solution:

Five ways to travel from City A to City P are:

1. A → B → P
2. A → C → P
3. A → B → C → P
4. A → D → E → P
5. A → D → E → C → P

Going from A to B and then to P is the best option.

Total distance traveled is the least.

11. 48 − 10 = 38

38 ÷ 2 = 19

19 + 10 = 29

The heavier goat is at least 29 kg.

Since the mass of the lighter goat is more than 16 kg, three possible masses of the heavier goat are 29 kg, 30 kg, or 31 kg.

12. 2 km 5 cm = 2 × 1,000 × 100 cm + 5 cm

= 200,000 cm + 5 cm

= 200,005 cm

13. 4,050 g = 4 kg 50 g

14. 750 mL = 0 L 750 mL

15. Step 1 Put two coins on each side of a balance. The lighter side contains the fake coin.

Step 2 Take the two coins from the lighter side and put one on each side of the balance. The fake coin will be on the lighter side.

Chapter 12

1. Thinking skill: Comparing

Solution:

Aiden's height → 136 cm − 25 cm

= 111 cm

Eric's height → 111 cm + 14 cm

= 125 cm

Eric is 1 meter 25 centimeters tall.

2. Thinking skill: Analyzing parts and whole

Solution:

62 m 36 cm = 6,236 cm

34 m 54 cm = 3,454 cm

6,236 − 3,454 = 2,782

2,782 cm = 27 m 82 cm

The car must travel 27 meters 82 centimeters.

3. Thinking skill: Analyzing parts and whole

Solution:

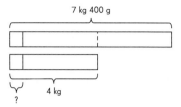

7 kg 400 g = 7,400 g

4 kg = 4,000 g

7,400 − 4,000 = 3,400

The mass of half of the paint is 3,400 grams.

4,000 − 3,400 = 600

The mass of the empty can is 600 grams.

4. Thinking skill: Analyzing parts and whole

Solution:

550 mL × 6 = 3,300 mL

= 3 L 300 mL

The total capacity is 3 liters 300 milliliters.

5. Thinking skill: Deduction

Solution:

4 × ☐ = 62 − 30

= 32

☐ = 32 ÷ 4

= 8

The mass of the suitcase is 8 kilograms.

6. Thinking skill: Analyzing parts and whole

Solution:

3 km 350 m = 3,350 m

2 km 420 m = 2,420 m

3,350 + 2,420 + 3,350 = 9,120

Xavier jogs 9,120 meters in all.

7. Thinking skill: Analyzing parts and whole

Solution:

Amount of lemonade sold on Tuesday is

3 L 596 mL − 679 mL = 2 L 917 mL

Amount of lemonade sold on Wednesday is

8 L − 3 L 596 mL − 2 L 917 mL

= 1 L 487 mL

8. Strategy: Use a diagram

Solution:

80 m

X X X X X X X X X X X

8 m

80 ÷ 8 = 10

10 + 1 = 11

11 × 2 = 22

There are 22 streetlamps altogether.

9. Strategy: Work backward

   Solution:
   500 × 4 = 2,000 mL or 2 L
   16 L + 2 L = 18 L
   18 L ÷ 3 = 6 L
   6 L × 4 = 24 L
   There was 24 liters of water in the tank at first.

10. Strategy: Use a model

    Solution:
    Mass of the items only = 66 kg − 4 kg
                                       = 62 kg

    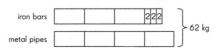

    62 kg − 6 kg = 56 kg
    7 units → 56 kg
    1 unit → 8 kg
    8 kg + 2 kg = 10 kg
    The mass of one iron bar is 10 kilograms, and the mass of one metal pipe is 8 kilograms.

11. Strategy: Use a model

    Solution:

    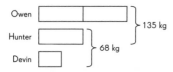

    3 units → 135 kg
    1 unit → 135 kg ÷ 3 = 45 kg
    Devin's mass = 68 kg − 45 kg
                          = 23 kilograms

12. Strategy: Use a model

    Solution:

    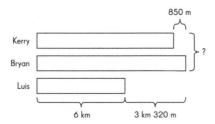

    Distance walked by Bryan:
    6 km + 3 km 320 m = 9 km 320 m
    Distance walked by Kerry:
    9 km 320 m − 850 m = 8 km 470 m
    Distance walked by Bryan and Kerry:
    9 km 320 m + 8 km 470 m
    = 17 km 790 m

13. Answers vary.

    Sample answer:
    a. There are two pencils.
       One pencil is 24 centimeters long.
       The other pencil is 2 centimeters shorter.
       What is the length of the shorter pencil?
       Solution: 24 cm − 2 cm = 22 cm
       The shorter pencil is 22 centimeters long.
    b. There are two pencils.
       One pencil is 24 centimeters long.
       The other pencil is 2 centimeters shorter.
       What is the total length of both pencils?
       Solution:
       24 cm − 2 cm = 22 cm
       22 cm + 24 cm = 46 cm
       Total length of both pencils is 46 centimeters.

14. Answers vary.

    Sample answer:
    There are 3 packets of flower seeds.
    Packet B's mass is 4 times as much as Packet
    A's mass. Packet C's mass is 16 grams less than
    Packet B's mass.
    Find the mass of Packet C.
    Solution:
    56 ÷ 9 = 8
    8 × 4 = 32
    32 − 16 = 16
    Packet C has a mass of 16 grams.

15. Answers vary.

    Sample answer:
    Augusta pours 725 milliliters of milk into a bottle
    from a jug.
    The jug is left with 248 milliliters of milk.
    How much milk was in the jug at first?
    Solution:
    725 mL + 248 mL = 973 mL
    There was 973 milliliters at first.

16. Answers vary.

    Sample answers:
    Bradley sells 4 times as much meat as Casper.
    They sell 25 kilograms of meat altogether.
    After selling, Casper has 7 kilograms of meat left.
    How much meat does each person have at first?
    Solution:
    Mass of meat Casper sells:
    25 kg ÷ 5 = 5 kg
    Mass of meat Casper had at first:
    5 kg + 7 kg = 12 kg
    Mass of meat Bradley had at first:
    5 kg × 4 = 20 kg

Chapter 13

1. Thinking skill: Comparing

   Solution: 15

2. Thinking skill: Comparing

   Solution: 20

3. Thinking skill: Comparing

   Solution: 75

4. Thinking skill: Analyzing parts and whole

   Solution: 110

5. Thinking skill: Analyzing parts and whole

   Solution: 40

6. Thinking skill: Analyzing parts and whole

   Solution: 9

7. Thinking skill: Comparing

   Solution:

   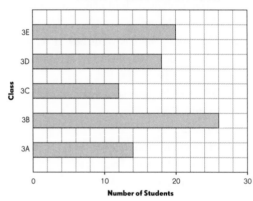

   Number of Students in Each Class

8. Thinking skill: Analyzing parts and whole

   Solution: 9

9. Thinking skill: Analyzing parts and whole

   Solution: 26

10. Thinking skill: Analyzing parts and whole

    Solution: 37

11. Thinking skill: Comparing

    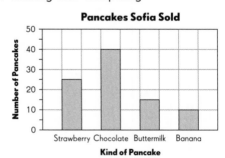

    Pancakes Sofia Sold

12. Thinking skills: Comparing, Analyzing parts and whole

    Solution: 33

13. Thinking skills: Comparing, Analyzing parts and whole

    Solution:

    Earnings from strawberry pancakes

    $3 × 25 = $75

    Earnings from chocolate pancakes

    $2 × 40 = $80

    She earns more from chocolate pancakes.

14. Thinking skills: Comparing, Analyzing parts and whole

    Solution:

    18 × 5 = 90

    155 − 90 = 65

    She needs to sell 65 more pancakes.

15. Thinking skill: Comparing

    Solution:

Number of Pencils	Tally	Number of Friends
1	~~HHH~~ ///	8
2	~~HHH~~	5
3	~~HHH~~ ~~HHH~~ ~~HHH~~ /	16
4	~~HHH~~ //	7
5	~~HHH~~ ~~HHH~~ //	12

Each **X** stands for 1 friend.

16. Thinking skill: Comparing

    Solution:

    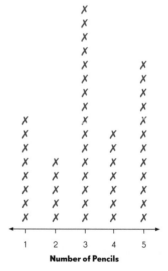

    Number of Pencils

17. Thinking skill: Comparing

    Solution: 19

18. Thinking skill: Comparing

    Solution: 7

19. Thinking skill: Comparing

    Solution: 29

20. Strategy: Look for patterns

    Solution:

    1, 1 + 2, 1 + 2 + 3, 1 + 2 + 3 + 4,
    1 + 2 + 3 + 4 + 5, ?
    1 + 2 + 3 + 4 + 5 + 6 = 21
    There will be 21 ✗s for 6 marbles.

21. Strategy: Use a diagram, Work backward

    Solution:

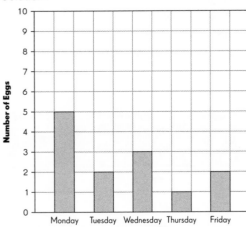

    Day of the Week

    Monday → 2 + 3 = 5
    Tuesday → 2
    Wednesday → 3
    Thursday → 5 − 4 = 1
    Friday → 2
    Eggs bought = 5 + 2 + 3 + 1 + 2 + 12
               = 25

    Gillian buys <u>25</u> eggs from the market.

22.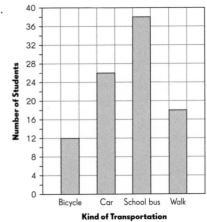

    Kind of Transportation

23.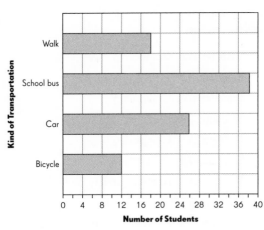

24. 2

25. Sylvia

26. 5

27. Answers vary.

    Sample answer:

    Q1: On which day did Bruce bake twice as
    many muffins as he baked on Wednesday?
    Answer: Monday

    Q2: How many muffins were baked on
    Wednesday and Thursday altogether?
    Answer: 39

    Q3: What is the fewest number of muffins baked
    in one day?
    Answer: 18

    Q4: How many more muffins were baked on
    Monday than on Thursday?
    Answer: 24

Chapter 14

1. Thinking skill: Comparing

    Solution: $\frac{6}{12}$; $\frac{2}{6}$; $\frac{4}{12}$

2. Thinking skill: Comparing

    Solution:

$\frac{6}{9}$	$\frac{2}{10}$	$\frac{1}{4}$
$\frac{4}{12}$	$\frac{2}{8}$	$\frac{3}{10}$
$\frac{6}{10}$	$\frac{4}{4}$	$\frac{11}{12}$
$\frac{1}{8}$	$\frac{5}{7}$	$\frac{4}{5}$

3. Thinking skill: Comparing

    Solution: $\frac{1}{6}$

4. Thinking skill: Deduction

    Solution: $\frac{1}{2} = \frac{4}{8} = \frac{6}{12}$

5. Thinking skill: Analyzing parts and whole

    Solution: $\frac{3}{4}$ of $12 = 9$

    9 parts need to be shaded to have $\frac{3}{4}$ of
    the figure shaded.

    $9 - 4 = 5$

    5 more parts need to be shaded.

6. Thinking skill: Analyzing parts and whole

    Solution:

    $\frac{3}{6} + \frac{5}{12}$

    $= \frac{6}{12} + \frac{5}{12}$

    $= \frac{11}{12}$

    $\frac{12}{12} - \frac{11}{12} = \frac{1}{12}$

    So, $\frac{1}{12}$ of the pole is not painted.

7. Strategy: Look for patterns

    Solution: $\frac{1}{4}$

8. Strategy: Work backward

    Solution:

    a. Total number of slices Sally, Henry, and
        Brenda have altogether

        $2 + 5 + 2 = 9$

        Since, Peter takes a quarter of the pie, this
        means that 9 slices is three-quarters. Thus, a
        quarter is 3 slices.

        $9 + 3 = 12$

        Brenda cuts the pie into 12 slices.

    b. $\frac{2}{12} = \frac{1}{6}$

        Brenda is left with $\frac{1}{6}$ of the pie.

9. Answers vary.

    Sample answer:

    Method 1

    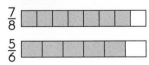

    $\frac{7}{8}$ is greater than $\frac{5}{6}$.

Method 2

$\frac{7}{8} = \frac{21}{24}$

$\frac{5}{6} = \frac{20}{24}$

Since $\frac{21}{24}$ is greater than $\frac{20}{24}$, $\frac{7}{8}$ is

greater than $\frac{5}{6}$.

10. $\frac{1}{4}$ of total number of fruits is 24.

    Total number of fruits picked is
    $24 \times 4 = 96$.

    $\frac{5}{9}$ of total number of fruits is

    $96 \times \frac{5}{9} = \frac{480}{9} = 53R3$

    Hector picked at least 54 fruits.

11. $\frac{5}{8}, \frac{7}{12}, \frac{1}{2}$

    Step 1 Use $\frac{1}{2}$ as the benchmark.

    Compare $\frac{5}{8}$ and $\frac{7}{12}$ with $\frac{1}{2}$.

    Both $\frac{5}{8}$ and $\frac{7}{12}$ are greater than $\frac{1}{2}$.

    Step 2 Compare $\frac{5}{8}$ and $\frac{7}{12}$ by making their

    denominators the same.

    $\frac{5}{8} = \frac{15}{24}$

    $\frac{7}{12} = \frac{14}{24}$

    $\frac{5}{8} > \frac{7}{12}$

    Step 3 Order the fractions from greatest to least.

    $\frac{5}{8}, \frac{7}{12}, \frac{1}{2}$

12. Step 1 Change the denominator 4 to 8
    by multiplying by 2.

    Step 2 Multiply the numerator by 2.

    $\frac{3}{4} = \frac{6}{8}$

    Step 3 Shade 6 of the 8 boxes.

13. Step 1 Change the denominator 14 to 7
    by dividing by 2.

    Step 2 Divide the numerator by 2.

    $\frac{6}{14} = \frac{3}{7}$

    Step 3 Shade 3 of the 7 boxes.

14. Compare the fraction $\frac{2}{5}$ with the benchmark $\frac{1}{2}$. $\frac{2}{5}$ is less than $\frac{1}{2}$.

$\frac{1}{2} + \frac{1}{3}$ will result in a fraction that is greater than $\frac{1}{2}$.

Since Jason's solution of $\frac{2}{5}$ is less than $\frac{1}{2}$, we know that his solution cannot be correct.

Chapter 15

1. Thinking skills: Comparing, Sequencing

Solution:

Dan's height ⟶ 51 in.
Carla's height ⟶ 51 in. + 3 in. = 54 in.
Boyle's height ⟶ 54 in. + 6 in. = 60 in.
Andy's height ⟶ 60 in. − 2 in. = 58 in.
Dan, Carla, Andy, Boyle

2. Thinking skill: Analyzing parts and whole

Solution:

3 gallons = 16 × 3 = 48 cups
2 quarts = 2 × 4 = 8 cups
4 pints = 2 × 4 = 8 cups
48 + 8 + 8 = 64
64 ÷ 4 = 16

16 bottles of water are needed to fill the container completely.

3. Thinking skill: Analyzing parts and whole

Solution:

7 × 3 = 21 oz
16 oz × 3 = 48 oz
48 − 21 = 27

◯ weighs 27 ounces.

4. Strategy: Use a model

Solution:

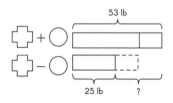

53 lb − 25 lb = 28 lb

5. Strategy: Simplify the problem

Solution:

2 quarts = 8 cups (syrup)
2 gallons = 32 cups (water)
1 cup of syrup and 4 cups of water serve 2 people.
8 cups of syrup and 32 cups of water serve 16 people.

6. Strategy: Use a diagram

Solution:

There are 8 intervals.
64 ÷ 8 = 8
Each interval is 8 yards long.
8 × 3 = 24
The distance between the 4th and the 7th street lamps is 24 yards.

7. Strategy: Use a model

Solution:

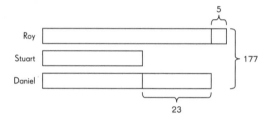

177 − 5 − 23 − 23 = 126
126 ÷ 3 = 42
Stuart jumps a distance of 42 inches.

8. Strategy: Work backward

Solution:

4 + 6 + 2 = 12
12 × 3 = 36
36 + 12 = 48
The truck had 48 pounds of flour to start with.

9. Routes to fly to City A from City C

Route	Distance (mi)
A ⟶ B ⟶ C	492 + 369 = 861
A ⟶ C	615
A ⟶ D ⟶ C	456 + 608 = 1,064
A ⟶ B ⟶ D ⟶ C	492 + 760 + 608 = 1,860

Route A to B to D to C covers the longest distance.

10. 2 gallons = 8 quarts

   2 gallons = 16 pints

Combinations	Quart container	Pint container
1	0	16
2	8	0
3	7	2
4	6	4
5	5	6
6	4	8

11. 1 mile 70 yards is not equal to 1,070 yards.

   1 mi = 1,760 yd

   So, 1 mi 70 yd = 1,760 yd + 70 yd

   $\qquad$ = 1,830 yd

   1 mile 70 yards is equal to = 1,830 yards.

12. 4 gallons is not equal to 2 × 4 pints.

   1 gallon = 8 pints

   4 gallons = 4 × 8 pints

   $\qquad$ = 32 pints

   4 gallons is equal to 32 pints.

13. 3 pounds is not equal to 3 × 12 ounces.

   1 pound = 16 ounces

   3 pounds = 3 × 16 ounces

   $\qquad$ = 48 ounces

   3 pounds is equal to 48 ounces.

14. **Step 1** Weigh two coins on a balance.

   Step 2 If the two coins weigh the same, the remaining coin weighs 2 ounces.

   Step 3 If the coins do not weigh the same, the one that weighs less is the 2 ounce coin.

15. 16 pints, 7 quarts, 1 gallon, 5 pints, 7 pints

   Step 1 Convert all the units to pints.

   Step 2 1 gallon 5 pints = 13 pints, 7 quarts = 14 pints

   Step 3 Order from smallest to largest.

Chapter 16

1. Thinking skill: Comparing

   Solution:

   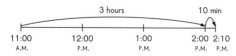

   3 h 10 min − 45 min = ?

   2 h 70 min

   2 h 70 min − 45 min = 2 h 25 min

   Vanessa studies for 2 hours 25 minutes.

2. Thinking skill: Analyzing parts and whole

   Solution:

   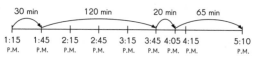

   She reaches the mall at 1:45 P.M.

   She leaves the mall at 4:05 P.M.

   The cab ride is 1 hour 5 minutes long.

3. Thinking skill: Comparing

   Solution:

   6 hours after 8:00 A.M. is 2:00 P.M.

   He leaves school at 2:00 P.M.

   1 hour 15 minutes after 2 P.M. is 3:15 P.M.

   He leaves the pool at 3:15 P.M.

4. Thinking skill: Comparing

   Solution:

   45 min + 20 min = 65 min = 1 h 5 min

   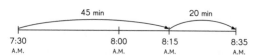

   1 hour 5 minutes after 7:30 A.M. is 8:35 A.M.

5. Thinking skill: Comparing

   Solution: 3 P.M.

6. Thinking skill: Comparing

   Solution: 11 P.M.

7. Thinking skill: Comparing

   Solution: 70°F

8. Thinking skill: Comparing

   Solution: 13°F

9. Strategy: Look for patterns

   Solution:

   The temperature increases by 13°F in an hour.

   71°F + 13°F + 13°F

   = 97°F

   The temperature would be 97°F at 6 P.M.

10. Strategy: Work backward

   Solution:

   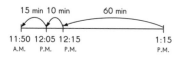

   They leave for the market at 11:50 A.M.

11. Answers vary.

Sample answer:
four forty-five; 4:45; 45 minutes past 4;
15 minutes to 5
Accept both A.M. and P.M. if given.

12. Answers vary.
Sample answer:
I have my lunch.
I take a nap.
I go swimming.
I play basketball.

13. **Method 1**

$10\ h\ 15\ min - 7\ h\ 55\ min = ?$

9 h 75 min
$9\ h\ 75\ min - 7\ h\ 55\ min = 2\ h\ 20\ min$
The movie was 2 hours 20 minutes long.

Method 2

```
        120 min      20 min
    ┌─────────────┬───────┐
  7:55         8:55    9:55 10:15
  P.M.         P.M.    P.M.  P.M.
```

$$120\ min + 20\ min = 2\ h + 20\ min$$
$$= 2\ h\ 20\ min$$

The movie was 2 hours 20 minutes long.

14. Mistake: The time shown is not half past 12.

Correct answer: The time shown on the clock is half past 1.

15. Mistake: The time shown on the clock is not 7:20.

Correct answer: The time shown on the clock is 4:35.

16. 225 min

Step 1 $3\ h \times 60 = 180\ min$

Step 2 $180\ min + 45\ min = 225\ min$

17. 1 h 40 min

Step 1 $100\ min = 60\ min + 40\ min$

Step 2 $60\ min + 40\ min = 1\ h\ 40\ min$

18. 4 h 15 min

Step 1 $4\ h \times 60 = 240\ min$
There are 4 hours in 240 minutes.

Step 2 $255\ min - 240\ min = 15\ min$

Chapter 17

1. Thinking skill: Spatial visualization
Solution:
U, O, Q, S

2. Thinking skill: Spatial visualization
Solution:
A, X, H

3. Thinking skill: Spatial visualization, Comparing
Solution:
$5 - 2 = 3$ more

4. Thinking skill: Spatial visualization, Classifying
Solution:

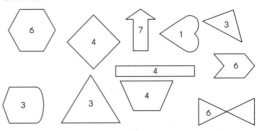

5. Thinking skill: Spatial visualization
Solution:
216
$9 \times 4 = 36$
$36 \times 6 = 216$

6. Solution:
Draw the figure to scale using centimeters.
Each side of the square is 4 centimeters and the base of the triangle is 6 centimeters.

7. Strategy: Look for patterns
Solution: $10 \times 2 = 20$
$20 - 2 = 18$
The 10th line will have 18 right angles.

8. Strategy: Look for pattern
Solution:
Pattern 1 has 4 right angles.
Pattern 2 has 12 right angles.
Pattern 3 has 20 right angles.
Pattern 4 has 28 right angles.
Pattern 5 has 36 right angles.

9. Answers vary.
Sample answer:

10. Answers vary.
    Sample answer:

11. No.

12.

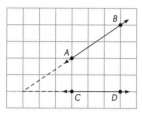

Point *B* is 4 square units away from point *D*.
Point *A* is 2 square units away from point *C*.
The distances between the lines are not the same.
So, line *AB* is not parallel to line *CD*.

OR

If you make line *AB* and line *CD* longer, they
will meet at a point.
Parallel lines never meet.
So, line *AB* is not parallel to line *CD*.

Chapter 18

1. Thinking skill: Spatial visualization
    Solution:
    Answers vary.
    Sample answer:

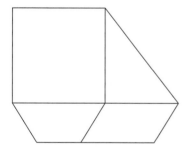

2. Thinking skill: Spatial visualization
    Solution:

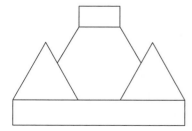

3. Thinking skill: Spatial visualization
    Solution:

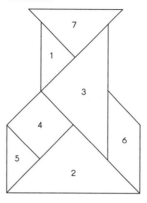

4. Strategy: Work backward
    Solution:

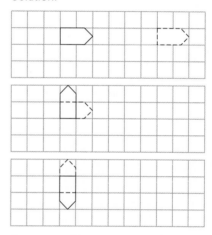

5. Strategies: Use a diagram, Look for patterns
    Solution: 27 (7 + 7 + 7 + 6)

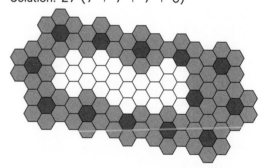

6. a. In both quadrilaterals, the opposite sides are
       parallel and equal in length.
    b. One pair of opposite sides is parallel.

7. a. Answers vary.
       Accept all figures that have the same shape
       and size.
    b. Answers vary.
       Accept all figures that have a different shape
       and/or size.

8.

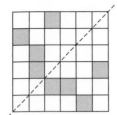

9. a. Both the shapes are facing the same direction.
       It is a slide, not a flip.
    b. The shape has changed position but it still
       faces the same direction.
       It is a slide, not a rotation.
    c. The shapes are facing different directions.
       It is a rotation, not a slide.
    d. The statement is true.

10. a. They are not the same shape or the same size.
    b. They are not the same size.

Chapter 19

1. Thinking skill: Spatial visualization
    Solution:

    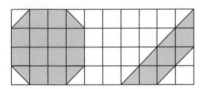

    2 + 8 + 10 = 20
    He must add 20 more squares.

2. Thinking skill: Spatial visualization
    Solution:
    5 − 3 = 2
    10 + 2 + 2 = 14
    8 + 2 + 2 = 12
    14 + 12 + 14 + 12 = 52
    The perimeter will be 52 centimeters.

3. Thinking skill: Spatial visualization
    Solution:
    8 ÷ 2 = 4
    6 ÷ 2 = 3
    4 × 3 = 12
    She can cut 12 squares from the paper.

4. Thinking skill: Spatial visualization
    Solution:
    6 + 6 + 6 + 6 = 24
    24 − 3 − 3 = 18
    18 ÷ 2 = 9
    The length of the rectangle is 9 feet.

5. Strategies: Work backward, Use a diagram
    Solution:
    E → 6 cm^2
    D → 6 cm^2
    C → 6 × 2 = 12 cm^2
    B → 12 × 2 = 24 cm^2
    A → 24 × 2 = 48 cm^2
    6 + 6 + 12 + 24 + 48 = 96 cm^2
    The area of the whole rectangle is 96 square
    centimeters.

6. Strategy: Look for patterns
    Solution:

    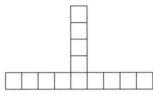

    The area of the 5th pattern is 13 square inches.

7. Answers vary.
    Sample answer:

    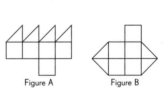

    Figure A   Figure B   Figure C

    The area for each figure is 7 square units but
    the perimeters for each figure vary.
    Figures can have the same area but different
    perimeters.

8. a. A → 1
       B → 3
       C → 6
    b. There are 10 squares in D.
    c. Yes.
    d. 55

9. | Step 1 | 54 − 15 − 15 = 24 |
    | Step 2 | 24 ÷ 2 = 12 |
    | Step 3 | The width of the rectangle is 12 centimeters. |

10. | Step 1 | Length of the rectangle = 27 − 15 = 12 cm |
    | Step 2 | 15 + 27 + 6 + 12 + 9 + 15 = 84 |
    | Step 3 | The perimeter of the figure is 84 centimeters. |